A WEEKEND WITH WINSLOW HOMER

A WEEKEND WITH
WINSLOW
HOMER

by Ann Keay Beneduce

RIZZOLI
NEW YORK

Come in, come in, don't be shy. I'm not as gruff as people say I am. It's just that sometimes I like to be alone, so I can paint in peace. And I'm never lonely here in my studio on the coast of Maine. Just look out that window and you'll understand. There's always something wonderful to see out there—the sun over the ocean, some fishermen hard at work. Or look out the other window—do you see those boys lying in a meadow? And beyond that, some young ladies are enjoying a game of croquet on the lawn in front of my brother's house. You know, some people say an artist has to live in Paris to be successful, but I've tried it, and I don't agree. My roots are here, in America. I have come to think that nature is the most inspiring subject of all for an artist, and I can get closer to nature right here than almost anywhere else in the world. But wait a moment—please don't move! The light is marvelous on your face! May I do a quick sketch of you? And after that I'll tell you how I got to be the most famous artist in America. Yes, that's who I am. I'm Winslow Homer.

Winslow Homer

There! That's finished! I enjoy drawing young people like you. They are the subjects of some of my best-known paintings and drawings. Perhaps it's because I had a happy childhood myself. I was born in Boston, but when I was six years old, our family—Mother, Father, and I, with my two brothers, Charles and Arthur—moved to Cambridge, a nearby suburb. Cambridge is like a city in itself now, but at that time it was really rural, with woods and fields for us to play in, the river for fishing and boating. What good times we had! Charlie and Arthur and I were not only brothers but also best friends, and, in fact, we've been that way ever since. We're a very close family. My father's a businessman and he's had some financial ups and downs, but I would say we were fairly comfortably off. Both my brothers also went into business, but that didn't appeal to me at all. I never wanted to be anything but an artist. I loved to draw, and my mother, who was very good at watercolors herself, encouraged me. I drew pictures of everything and everyone—of my brothers, of friends, of trees and farmhouses, dogs and cows—I was *always* drawing.

Portrait of Arthur B Homer — Bu Winslow

Then one morning at breakfast, my father noticed an ad in the newspaper. He read it out loud: "Boy wanted, apply to Bufford. . . . Must have a taste for drawing. No other wanted." J. H. Bufford was the owner of a printing business in Boston, and the position he offered sounded like a splendid opportunity for me, so I answered the ad. At first Mr. Bufford gave me some free-lance work to do—illustrating sheet-music covers for popular songs. The first two of these, "O Whistle and I'll Come to You" and "Katy Darling," came out in 1854, when I was just eighteen years old. Can you imagine how proud my family was to have these sitting on the music rack of our piano?!

Mr. Bufford must have been pleased, too, for soon afterward he signed me on as an apprentice, with a two-year contract, to perfect my skill as an illustrator. This was not a paying job; in fact, I had to pay *him* for the privilege of learning his craft. And it was very hard work—ten hours a day. It soon began to feel to me like slavery. At the end of my agreed-upon two years, on my twenty-first birthday, I declared my independence and left Bufford's. What a relief! I swore then that I'd never again call any man my master—and I never have, to this day!

But my time at Bufford's wasn't wasted, for many people had seen the pictures I did there, and soon I began getting jobs doing original drawings for other Boston publications, like *Ballou's Pictorial Drawing Room Companion*. At that time, photography was a rather new invention and not widely used. Instead, newspapers and journals relied on artists like me to provide their illustrations. Soon the editors of *Harper's Weekly,* down in New York, noticed my work, which, if I must say so myself, was much livelier than that of most of my colleagues, and they asked me to do some drawings for them. Before long, I was doing so many pictures for *Harper's Weekly* that I decided to move to New York City. I was becoming very well known—in fact, some people said I was the best illustrator in the country. How were my pictures printed in the magazines and newspapers, you ask? Well, it is interesting—they were prepared for printing by a method known as wood engraving. A block of wood would be cut to the size needed. Then the surface of one end would be sanded very smooth and painted white. Sometimes I would draw my picture right on this surface—or sometimes I drew it in ink on a piece of paper and

BALLOU'S PICTORIAL

M. M. BALLOU, { NUMBER 22 WINTER STREET.   BOSTON, SATURDAY, JUNE 13, 1857. $3 00 PER ANNUM. 6 CENTS SINGLE. } VOL. XII., No. 24.——WHOLE No. 312.

CORNER OF WASHINGTON AND SUMMER STREETS.

The local view upon this page, drawn expressly for us by Mr. Winslow Homer, a promising young artist of this city, is exceedingly faithful in architectural detail and spirited in character, and represents one of the busiest and most brilliant spots in all Boston. The sketch is made from the north sidewalk of Winter Street. The most prominent building in the view is the large stone structure at the corner of Washington and Summer Streets, the lower story of which is occupied by the magnificent jewelry establishment of Messrs. Jones, Shreve, Brown & Co., and which vies in splendor and attraction with similar magazines in New York, London or Paris. This is always an attractive spot, and you can scarcely pass it any hour of the day without finding loiterers at the windows, with bright eyes gazing on the kindred diamonds, or scanning the superb plate, watches and rings there displayed in dazzling profusion. Within, the elegant arrangements, the spacious

counters, the lofty groined ceiling and all the appointments harmonize well with the character of the business. Opposite this establishment is that of Orlando Tompkins, apothecary, which has recently been refitted and renovated in the style of the Renaissance, with carving, gilding, fresco-painting, mirrors, marble, etc., in the most approved style of luxury. We merely show the corner of this store. The name of George Turnbull appears upon the awning in front of his store, No. 5 and 7 Winter Street, which projected within our artist's field of vision. Turnbull's is another noted Boston establishment, and a fine specimen of the retail dry goods store. It is a favorite resort of ladies, who are attracted by the complete assortment of goods always found there, and the politeness and attention with which their wants are supplied. Mr. Turnbull enjoys an enviable reputation, and conducts a very extensive business. The figures introduced in our sketch, give a good idea of the character and bustle of this part of the city in the

busiest part of the day. Here we have a carriage dashing up at rather an illegal rate of speed which might endanger the lady at the crossing, but for the gentlemanly policeman who is stationed here to ensure the safety of pedestrians and moderate the ardor of charioteers, and who steps forward to lend his assistance and interpose his potential authority. In another place we have an itinerant Italian with his organ, on the summit of which resides habitually a painful caricature of humanity in the guise of a monkey, attired in shabby habiliments, whose chief offices are to hold his hat for money and amuse the juveniles with his antic capers. Promenaders of both sexes, and pedestrians of all ages, complete the lively picture. At this point, Washington Street presents many of the characteristics of Broadway, New York. In the human tide that pours through it there is nearly the same diversity of feature and origin, and the amount of passing is perhaps larger in proportion to the size of the city, crowding the sidewalks full.

CORNER OF WINTER, WASHINGTON AND SUMMER STREETS, BOSTON.

transferred it to the woodblock. Now the engraver had to cut away the wood from the lines, removing only the white areas, so the black lines of the drawing remained raised. When the ink was applied to the raised areas and paper was rolled or pressed over them, the image was printed on the paper—but in *reverse*. The type that was used to print the news items or stories was also raised, so the pictures and text could be printed at the same time. I never actually had to do the wood engraving myself—this was the work of highly skilled craftsmen, but it was a tedious job and I preferred to spend my time more creatively, producing the original drawings. Artists who could do lively and appealing—and accurate—drawings for wood engravings were in great demand, so I had plenty of work to do.

Croquet Scene: *This appealing oil painting was completed in 1866, the same year in which Homer's painting* Prisoners from the Front *brought the young artist his first taste of fame. Here he has made use of the strong contrast between the dark background and the whites and bright colors of the women's dresses to catch and hold the viewer's attention.*

One of my more exciting assignments was doing sketches of the inauguration of President Lincoln for *Harper's Weekly*. Then, in the fall of 1861 and again in the spring of 1862, *Harper's* sent me to cover some of the activities of the Union troops in the Civil War. I followed General McClellan's Army of the Potomac on a campaign and sketched my impressions. I also made many sketches at the siege of Yorktown, and once back in my studio, I made finished drawings for the magazine from them. Until then, I had mainly illustrated scenes from pleasant upper-class life. True, I had always tried to draw them just as they were, without trying to "prettify" them. But the Civil War evoked sharper, deeper, and more painful emotions and images. In the battle scenes, my ability to sketch quickly and accurately enabled me to catch the action convincingly. At first I found this very exciting. However, as you can imagine, the violence was also disturbing, and I began to prefer showing quieter scenes—soldiers in camp, dreaming of home, or cheering each other up with improvised entertainments. My *Harper's* illustrations based on these Civil War sketches were very popular.

But illustrating was not my only goal, even though it had begun to bring me quite a good living. I really wanted to become a painter. When I got back to New York, I took four lessons from a French artist living there, just to learn how to get started. The rest was up to me. The first two oils that I did were of army life, based on sketches I had done at the front. One painting was called *The Sharpshooter*. (Here is a wood engraving of a drawing I made of the same soldier.) The other was called *Punishment for Intoxication*. These paintings were exhibited at the National Academy of Design in 1863. People were astonished that I had bloomed so quickly as a painter in oils. But, of course, I had already become very skillful at drawing—the essence of a good painting. And I had also developed a keen eye for composition—that is, for arranging the shapes and colors in a picture so that they formed a balanced and unified design. Perhaps my paints were put on a bit crudely at first, but the overall effect was appealing, according to critics.

However, in spite of this critical approval, I was still very unsure about whether or not I would be taken seriously as an artist. *Harper's* had made me a very generous offer to take a permanent position with them as an illustrator, and I wrote to my brother Charlie that if these two oil paintings did not sell,

I would give up painting and accept their offer. Now I'll tell you something that not many people know. Charlie understood how much I really wanted to become a painter, so, although he didn't have much money himself at the time, he secretly bought the two paintings through a dealer, making him promise not to tell me about it. I didn't discover who the real buyer was for years, but one night when I went to Charlie's house, I saw one of these paintings hanging on the wall! Well, he finally confessed that he was my secret benefactor. What a good brother! And yet, do you know, I was angry with him at first. I guess my pride was hurt. But of course my life would have been quite different if those two paintings had not been sold. As it was, I was able to decline *Harper's* offer and continue to work on my oil paintings.

Three years later, I finished and showed another Civil War painting, also at the National Academy of Design. It was called *Prisoners from the Front,* and it was an instant success. It is this picture that first made me really famous as an artist, not just as an illustrator. One critic called it the most important single painting of the war! It was soon sold, and after this I had somewhat fewer financial worries. Of course, this was gratifying, but what pleased me even more was that all this recognition was given to a painting that was not at all like the typical paintings that were in fashion at the time. It hadn't a trace of their sentimentality. It was straightforward realism, as close to the truth as I could make it. The image of the young officer receiving his prisoners is moving precisely because it is not sentimentalized; it reflects a real emotion, with dignity.

I felt that we Americans should stop thinking that European art and culture were somehow better than ours. I wanted to show the integrity and beauty of our own people and our own country in a very realistic, natural way. So the success of this painting was very encouraging for me. (Actually, though, by now I am

Homer (at left) and his friend Albert Kelsey in Paris, 1867. While in France, Homer did engravings of Parisian life for Harper's *like* A Parisian Ball *on the next page.*

a little tired of this particular painting! People who don't understand my more recent work keep asking me when I am going to do another painting like *Prisoners from the Front.* But a real artist doesn't want to go on working in the same style or on the same subject. There are always new challenges, new problems to work out, exciting new ways of seeing.)

Not long after this success, two of my paintings were accepted for exhibition in the International Exposition in Paris! You can imagine how honored I felt. It was the beginning of international recognition for my work. Then my friend Albert Kelsey suggested that we go and paint in Paris for a while "to follow the paintings," as he put it. Well, how could I resist? After all, Paris was considered the capital of the art world at that time, and all sorts of interesting painters, like Bougereau, Courbet, and Manet, were beginning to paint in a new way. Of course I wanted to see this excitement (not to mention the pretty Parisian girls), for myself! We stayed for ten months and worked very hard, as you can see by the bags under our eyes in

the photo of Albert and me—and by the drawings I sent back to *Harper's* showing our activities! But seriously, what I saw there had little real effect on my painting. I did some paintings in Paris and also in Picardy, sixteen or seventeen in all. I even did a painting on the wall of an inn in Cernay-la-Ville, in payment for a good meal. It's probably still there today! But I wasn't interested in the work of most of the French painters, and only Eugène Boudin, with whose work I was already familiar before I went to France, had much influence on my own art at that time. A "naturalist" painter, Boudin did some paintings of charmingly dressed socialites on fashionable beaches. I liked the way he grouped these figures, lit from behind by the reflected light of the sea and sky. He painted out-of-doors and caught the effects of sunlight, sea, and atmosphere with quick brush strokes. His paintings had a sort of rough, dry look that I liked; it seemed to me they looked more natural and real than the works of the more famous painters. I had done some paintings in a style similar to Boudin's,

but in American settings, of course. *Long Branch, New Jersey* is one of these.

Back home, I became more convinced than ever that, as an American artist, I should depend on my native land and people for my inspiration and should not try to imitate European masters. But perhaps my French experience *had* influenced me a little after all, for at least one critic said he had found a gayer, more fashionable mood in some of my new paintings. I don't agree with him, personally, for I claim that I was *always* interested in pretty young women and their fashions. One young woman, in particular, I have never forgotten, though I was not in a position to ask her to marry me then. She was the subject of many of my sketches and drawings. But she finally married another man. Maybe I'll show you a painting of her, which I have kept in my studio all these years. But you must promise not to tell anyone about this romantic disappointment of mine. It is a secret between you and me.... I've never shared it with anyone else, though my brothers suspected it.

Artistically, however, the next fourteen years were among my most productive ever. I threw myself into my work. I was probably not really suited to settled married life anyhow, as I was so intensely preoccupied with my art. I traveled a great deal during this period, too, visiting many parts of the Northeast: the Adirondacks, the Catskills, the New Jersey Shore, Pennsylvania, Long Island, and all parts of New England. Gradually, I began to find myself doing fewer paintings and drawings of colorful scenes of the pastimes of polite society—ladies playing croquet on well-kept lawns, or upper-class families vacationing at fashionable beach resorts in New Jersey or Long Island. Instead, I was drawn to a more serious, more typically American subject matter—farmers and their families at work, Adirondack guides and mountaineers, and men who lived by hunting and fishing as well as those who lived by the sea—fishermen, sailors, boat builders. All of these

In spite of the influence of Boudin, you can see that this painting, Long Branch, New Jersey, *is unmistakably Homer's. He has given it a strong, carefully planned composition and has brought the main figures forward, into the foreground. The woman in the white dress catches one's eye first because she is near the center and because the woman on the far right leans toward her. The tonal contrasts also make her stand out the most. Her dress is the whitest area in the painting, and is contrasted with the dark grass at the cliff's edge and her own dark sash and shadow. The line of other figures in the distance makes you then look to the left and down the steep stairs to a cottage. Other structures then curve around the lower left corner, leading you to the line of the cliff edge on the right and back to the main figures again.*

people were deeply involved with, and dependent upon, the many changing
moods of nature, the seasons, and the weather. I had never really liked doing
city scenes. Instead, I wanted to portray simple, hard-working people, with
dignity and character, in country settings of natural beauty. And I wanted to
do this as honestly as I possibly could. I really admired these people, so self-
reliant and courageous, wresting a hard but satisfying living from nature—
the land, the sea, the wilderness. I liked the idea of showing people at
work. And, of course, I relished the idea of painting nature, not just as a
background, but as an actor with a dynamic role, interacting with the other
players in the scene.

Does this all sound rather heavy and dark and serious to you? I don't mean
it to, but as I told you, I'm not used to talking so much about my private
thoughts, and perhaps I didn't express myself just right. For my paintings
of this period are not at all heavy and dark; they are probably the happiest
and brightest of all my work. I didn't limit my subject to men at work; in
fact, I often painted sturdy young farm women or rural schoolteachers, for

instance, or children at play. In 1870, I spent a wonderful summer in the Adirondack Mountains, camping, hiking, canoeing, fishing, and sketching, sketching, sketching. Then in the winter, back in my studio in New York, I made paintings (and drawings for wood engravings) from these sketches. Sometimes I visited farms or spent a few weeks at the seashore, sketching and observing. Sometimes I would see children absorbed in activities that seemed to hint at what kind of work they would do as adults, like the boy who has made a toy sailboat modeled on a real boat that is being built in the background; or a girl caring for a tiny, sick baby chick with maternal tenderness; or young people picking berries. All these sketches I would turn into drawings for wood engravings, or into paintings in oil or watercolor.

At this time, even though I hoped to become a great painter, I still depended for a living on the drawings that I could sell to be printed in *Harper's Weekly* and other such publications. But something new was about to enter my work! In 1873, I saw an exhibition of some excellent English

watercolors. Of course, I had been doing watercolors and wash drawings myself for many years, but I had somehow thought of them as minor works. A lot of them were done as color sketches before doing an oil painting or a wood engraving. But suddenly I realized that a well-done watercolor was a work of art in itself, and that there were effects that could be achieved in this medium that would be impossible in any other. Most of my earlier watercolors were done in opaque color, or colors mixed with white to get different tones. Now I began to experiment with transparent colors, letting the white of the paper shine through to provide the lighter tones. The results were exhilarating!

I had always preferred paintings that were really done out-of-doors. Trying to reproduce the effect of sunlight in my studio, working in oil on canvas from sketches done outside, had never fully satisfied me. But unlike oils, watercolors were light and easy to carry. I could take them with me and complete a painting at the seaside or in a meadow. What sparkling waves, what delicate lights and shadows I could now create! In that first year of serious work in this medium, I did a watercolor called *Berry Pickers* that is still one of my favorites. I also did a version of this for a wood engraving, which is reversed, as you can see, in the print made from the engraving. I added a figure at the left, so the print is not exactly a mirror image

of the watercolor, but both are based on the same sketch. In Gloucester, Massachusetts, and in Walden, New York (where I frequently visited Charlie's friend Lawton Valentine at his summer house), I began to work very seriously in watercolor. What a happy period it was for me! A few years later, Valentine and his family bought a place in Mountainville, New York, which they called Houghton Farm (Houghton was his wife's maiden name). They invited me there often and gave me great freedom to do my work. The children of the working farmers often posed for me, sometimes in their own everyday clothes, sometimes in costumes I brought with me. I particularly fancied having one or another of the girls pose as a shepherdess, wearing a ruffled cotton dress and a beribboned straw bonnet. These "American shepherdess" pictures were very popular as watercolors and were often reproduced as wood engravings in *Harper's Weekly,* too. Recalling my own happy boyhood with my brothers, I also painted some scenes of boys playing games, fishing, or just sitting in a pasture, talking and dreaming. When these watercolors were exhibited at the National Academy, the critics finally agreed that they were outstanding—the work of a home-grown American Impressionist. Indeed, I began to think that, in the future, I would be remembered chiefly for my watercolors rather than my oil paintings.

Do you know why they called me an Impressionist? There was at that time a very popular group of French painters who called themselves by this name. They preferred to paint outdoors rather than inside their studios, just as I did. In their paintings they tried to capture the impression of the varied and beautiful effects of light on the ocean and sky, on fields and gardens, on flowers, figures, and faces. So it is true that I shared a lot of their ideas—but I arrived at them by myself.

This is one of the charming American shepherdesses Homer painted at Houghton Farm, an exquisite watercolor in his newfound style. True, you can still see some opaque colors—he was just beginning to trust himself with transparent colors—but see how he has let the paper show through to create the effect of sunlight and pale, delicate shadows. The composition is simple and strong, all lines leading the eye to the central figure, a young girl. One can almost feel the warmth of the sunlight, and the gentle touch of the breeze that lifts the ribbons of her bonnet and the sheer ruffles of her dress.

I also did a lot of successful seaside scenes in Gloucester, as I mentioned to you. Among the best known of these was one showing a happy group of boys and one man sailing a small catboat in a rising breeze. I did a watercolor of this in 1873. Then I did an oil sketch of it, and finally a finished oil painting called *Breezing Up* or *A Fair Wind,* which was shown at the National Academy. Lawton Valentine loved it and wanted to buy it, but I didn't feel at the time that it was one of my best works and discouraged him from doing so. Someone else bought it, and to my surprise it has become one of my most popular works. Lawton had to settle for the oil sketch, which is actually quite fine, I must admit.

Ever since the Civil War, I had been deeply interested in the lives of the

former slaves, now freed. I had come to know some of the black soldiers who served with the Union Army when I was sketching at the front during the war. What were their lives like a decade later? In 1875, I went back to Petersburg, Virginia, to find out for myself. Some popular painters had already produced many pictures of plantation life, which I now saw were full of stereotypes. I was determined to show these people as they really were, not as types but as individuals, with warmth and dignity. The pictures I did then were generally well received later by the public, but while I was doing them it was a different story. Southern plantation owners were still suffering from their defeat. At one point a group of angry young white men threatened to run me out of town.

By this time, I was beginning to do well enough by my painting that I felt it would be safe to give up my work as an illustrator for *Harper's*. I handed in my last drawing to them in 1875. After that, I did do some illustrations for various publications from time to time, but I no longer thought of myself as anything but a painter.

As the 1870s drew to a close, I began to feel discontented with myself and my work. You've heard of "writer's block," I'm sure, haven't you? Well, I was having a sort of "artist's block." In spite of the popularity of my recent work, especially the watercolors of shepherdesses and happy children in pleasant outdoor settings, I was dissatisfied. I felt I needed a deeper, more serious subject, especially for my oil paintings. People were still calling me "a promising young artist," but I was really approaching middle age. I needed to be alone, to think about my work. I began to avoid my artist friends because I didn't want to hear their comments. My brother Charlie was now married; he and his wife and several other members of my family had summer homes here in Prout's Neck, Maine. Charlie offered me this studio on his property, and I gladly took refuge here in the summer, for months at a time. Yes, this same studio where you and I are talking today. But it was smaller then, and I did not live in it all year round as I do now. Even here, my privacy was often invaded by summer visitors who couldn't resist trying to meet "the famous artist." To scare off persistent ladies, I put up warnings of SNAKES! and MICE!—and, when I heard that my father planned a visit, I put up a sign COAL BIN, hoping the old man would be fooled by it and pass on by my little studio. I even frightened the well-meaning maid Charlie's wife had sent down to clean my studio by writing in big letters on my wall: LEAVE THIS ROOM!!

Finally, I decided I would have to go away by myself, somewhere where I didn't know anyone, where I could find the inspiration I needed to go on with my work. I had heard of Tynemouth, a village in England, on the coast of the North Sea. One of my artist friends in New York had mentioned that it was ruggedly beautiful. So in March of 1881 I set sail for England. Soon I was settled in a small cottage (with a high wall for privacy) in the nearby fishing village of Cullercoats. And here at last I found the subject matter I had been looking for. I had always liked to paint people enjoying themselves in nature. But here I found a much deeper drama—not scenes of children and pretty women enjoying themselves in sunny fields and woodlands, but strong men and women battling the treacherous sea for their livelihood, and sometimes for their very lives. Here was as heroic a theme as I could wish for.

For twenty months, I stayed in Cullercoats, painting in both watercolors and oils. New colors, darker and less sunny, began to appear in these works. Playful children disappeared. Men were no longer sailing for pleasure but pitting their courage and skill against the sea, an opponent much stronger

than themselves. And the women! These were not the dainty creatures I had become known for portraying but statuesque, sturdy women capable of working hard beside their men, unloading the catch, hauling in and mending the nets. Many of the best paintings I did at this time were of these women. And I took home with me many more sketches and ideas for paintings to be finished in the years to come.

When I stepped off the ship that brought me back to New York, I had no money left at all—not even enough to get to my studio! But I had high hopes for my Tynemouth works, and so did the owners of my gallery, Knoedler's; they sent a representative to meet me with cab fare. It is annoying to be constantly in need of money! I think of painting as my "business," and I am considered quite successful—yet I really think I earn less than a clerk in a store.

Well, fortunately, my new paintings, when they were shown, seemed to please most people. The critics praised the new strength and drama in my work. One of my Tynemouth paintings, however, didn't please the critics when I showed it at the National Academy in 1883. This was a painting I called *Coming Away of the Gale,* which showed a young fisherman's wife, with a baby tied in her shawl, striding toward a lifeguard station in a storm. Though I had composed the picture carefully, critics thought the lifeguard station was too prominent and that it took the viewer's attention away from what was supposed to be the main subject. I was terribly disappointed by this criticism. I let people think I had destroyed the painting. Ten years later—only recently, in fact—I showed another version of it at the Columbian Exposition in Chicago, minus the lifeguard station and a boat and some fishermen that were in the earlier one. In their places were some rocks and breaking waves. The new painting was narrower than the other one, too, and was called simply *The Gale.* This time I received the gold medal for it! Now I'll tell you another secret: This was not a new painting at all! I simply cut down the canvas a little at the left, so the woman is more centered on it. And then I painted out the lifeguard station, the fishermen, and the boat and put in the rocks and waves instead! The critics were right, I have to admit. The composition is very good now, don't you agree? In fact, this is one of my favorite paintings from that period.

The year after my return from England, I decided to leave New York for good. I was well-enough known to let my dealers present and sell my works for me. And I still felt the need for ready access to nature and for privacy to work. I settled into my studio here in Prout's Neck as my permanent home, though I still travel a lot. It is wonderful to have my family so near, especially my brother Charles and his wife, Mattie. All of us have remained close all our lives. My studio wasn't always just as you see it now. Charlie had it enlarged, so I'd have more room, and moved it so I could have this good north light and a beautiful view of the ocean.

Members of the Homer family having a corn roast at Prout's Neck, about 1900 (above), and Winslow Homer and his brother, Charles Savage Homer, Jr., showing off their catch (opposite).

Soon after my return from England, I exhibited an oil painting, *Lifeline,* in New York. On the very first day of the show, a collector bought it for $2,500. I was so excited, I rushed home to tell my mother the good news. People began referring to me as America's greatest painter! You can imagine how pleased my mother was! She was getting old; in fact, she died quite soon after this. I was glad she lived long enough to enjoy my success. She had believed in me through all the hard times.

Now, at last, style and subject matter seemed to be coming together for me. Several times I was able to go out with the fishing fleet to the Grand Banks off the coast of New England. Many good paintings came out of these trips. As in my Tynemouth paintings, I kept my compositions simple, with usually just one or a few large figures in the foreground. Though they were based on real individuals, I was trying to achieve a sort of universal effect also. There is a woman being rescued in *Lifeline,* but women as subjects were vanishing gradually from my newer work. Men and the sea appeared more and more often. Sometimes I would paint just the power of the sea itself. Man and the sea is certainly the subject of one of my most famous paintings, *The Gulf Stream.* I'm sure you know this one. It took me several years to complete. I have gone to Nassau, Cuba, and Bermuda several times in the past few years, partly to avoid the cold Maine winter. Have you ever been to these places? I was dazzled by the sunlight sparkling on the sea, by the brilliantly colorful tropical flowers and the palm trees, by the blues, greens, and violets of the water. I admired the men, with their muscular mahogany-colored bodies, who sailed and fished from graceful white sailboats or caught turtles for the market. I brought out my watercolors and my brushes and began to paint in a way that was entirely new to me—directly with my brushes, without making a drawing first—just a few sketchy lines to indicate my composition. I found that all my years of careful observation and drawing had trained my eyes and hand so that I could now paint with complete freedom and assurance. I got fatter brushes and used broader strokes, brighter colors.

Most of Homer's paintings of fishermen have less exotic settings than The Gulf Stream. In Eight Bells, *for instance, he shows two New England fishermen with navigating instruments in their hands. The wind is brisk, the sea is rough, but you can see that these men feel confident in their ability to guide the ship safely home.*

I worked quickly, so as to capture the effect of the sunlight and the reflected light of sea and sky. The watercolors I did in these tropical islands were extremely popular and sold very well.

But the southern sea was not always so calm—it could be dangerous, too. Sometimes there were waterspouts or raging hurricanes; and beneath the surface, hungry sharks awaited the unwary. I did several watercolors on the theme of an exhausted sailor on a storm-ravaged boat before I painted *The Gulf Stream* in oils. When I exhibited the painting in New York, the art critics declared that it was an American masterpiece—but many of the ordinary viewers found it disturbing. They thought it brutal or depressing. They were getting totally involved in the story the painting told, instead of appreciating how well it was painted. I was exasperated by them. Finally, I wrote to my dealer: "The criticisms...by old women and others are noted. You may inform these people that [the sailor] did not starve to death. He was not eaten by the sharks. The waterspout did not hit him. And he was rescued by a passing ship." My dealer thought I was a bit sarcastic. Well, you have seen the picture. What do *you* think will happen to him? He has at least survived the storm. But you can see that, even here, nature is not always benign and smiling. And the sea can be a dangerous adversary!

The Fox Hunt *is another example of a painting of nature without people. It was painted in Prout's Neck during a bitterly cold winter and reflects a sharp sense of Homer's isolation there. The fox is the prey; the hunters are the black crows, who are about to attack it. This scene is based on an incident the artist actually saw. As with* The Gulf Stream, *he has left the outcome to the viewer's imagination.*

Looking back over my work, now that I am getting on in years, I can see a sort of pattern in it, a constant theme that runs through all the many changes in style, medium, and subject matter. As I told you when we first met, I have always loved nature and the outdoors. I loved playing outdoors as a child—fishing and swimming, hiking and sailing, playing games with my brothers and friends. Nature was a paradise to be explored and enjoyed. You must know that feeling, too, don't you? I tried to show and share this remembered happiness in many of my early drawings and paintings. As a young man, I was also interested in showing the activities of other young men and women my age outdoors—perhaps on vacation. For a long time I continued to paint people enjoying nature, and some of my best and most popular works were on this theme. In them I tried to show the beauty of the American wilderness, the rustic charm of farm life, the pleasures of the seashore.

But my stay in England changed all that. Nature in Tynemouth was neither smiling nor sunny. The fishermen there had to struggle against an elemental force much stronger than they. Nature had always been at the heart of my work. Now it seemed to be testing me as a person and as an artist. People against nature, heroic people against the awesome power of the ocean, became my theme. My challenge was to express it. But in my recent works here in Maine, I have gone beyond that. People have almost disappeared from my paintings. Nature, however, remains. What I am trying to paint now is the power of the ocean itself, crashing on the rocks with enormous force, ever renewing itself....

Just listen to it roaring right now! There's a storm coming up—a real Northeaster! Did you bring your boots and your raincoat? Good! I'll put on my slicker, too. Let's go and look at the ocean.... Hurry! Hurry! It's just superb!

WHERE TO SEE HOMER

Fortunately for you, this great American master worked so passionately at his art that he produced a large body of work, not only oil paintings and watercolors, but also drawings, sketches, and other graphic works. This fact, in addition to his widespread popularity, has meant that there is scarcely a museum in any part of the United States where you cannot view some of his works. Many private collections also include his original drawings and paintings, and his wood engravings and other illustrations have been widely reproduced. Listed here are but some of the places where you can see Winslow Homer.

Arizona

The Phoenix Art Museum has some paintings and engravings, and the Arizona State University Art Museum in Tempe has an oil painting and a watercolor.

California

Each of the following museums has one or more Homers on view: Mills College Art Gallery, Oakland; San Diego Museum of Art; the M. H. de Young Memorial Museum in San Francisco; the Santa Barbara Museum of Art; the Galleries of the Claremont Colleges, Claremont; and the Los Angeles County Museum of Art.

Colorado

The Denver Art Museum has the oil painting *Two Figures by the Sea,* also called *The Storm.*

Connecticut

Some fine Homers can be seen in The Wadsworth-Atheneum, Hartford; The New Britain Museum of American Art; The Lyman Allyn Museum, New London; and Yale University Art Gallery, New Haven.

Delaware

The Delaware Art Museum, Wilmington, has an oil painting, *Milking Time*, that is related to several other Homer works.

District of Columbia

The following museums in Washington have several examples of Homer's work: The Corcoran Gallery of Art; The Freer Gallery of Art, Smithsonian Institution; The National Museum of American Art, Smithsonian Institution; The National Gallery of Art; and The Phillips Collection. In the collection at The National Gallery, you can see *Breezing Up (A Fair Wind)* and *Right and Left,* two of his most important oils, as well as some of his best-known watercolors, but you will find many appealing Homer paintings at the other museums also. Most of these museums are within walking distance of each other.

Florida

The Cummer Gallery of Art, Jacksonville, and The Norton Gallery of Art in West Palm Beach each have several Homers.

Georgia

The Georgia Museum of Art at the University of Georgia in Athens has a delightful watercolor, *A Sunflower for the Teacher.*

Illinois

The Krannert Art Museum at the University of Illinois in Champaign-Urbana has an oil painting done by Homer while he was in France. The Art Institute of Chicago has fine examples of Homer's oils and many outstanding watercolors, drawings, and sketches from all periods of his work. These include *The Gulf Stream, Flamborough Head,* and *For to Be a Farmer's Boy.* The Terra Museum of American Art, also in Chicago, has some of his important late oils.

Indiana

The Indianapolis Museum of Art has an oil painting of *Boat Builders* and several excellent watercolors.

Iowa

The Davenport Museum of Art and the Des Moines Art Gallery each have at least one work by Homer.

Kansas

Wichita Art Museum has an oil painting, and the Spencer Museum of Art at the University of Kansas in Lawrence has an oil and several Homer watercolors.

Kentucky

The J. B. Speed Art Museum, Louisville, has a watercolor, *The Schoolmistress.*

Maine

As you might expect, since so much of Winslow Homer's life was spent in Maine, there are good collections of his art in several museums here. Bowdoin College Museum of Art in Brunswick has some oils and some fine watercolors and drawings, including *Adolescence,* said to have been drawn when Homer was only ten years old. The museum also has many personal photographs of the artist and his family, plus letters and other memorabilia. The Portland Museum of Art owns at least one work by Homer. In Rockland, the William A. Farnsworth Library and Art Museum has some watercolors. In Waterville, the Colby College Museum of Art has *Portrait of Pauline* and *Trapper.*

Maryland

Some Homers may be seen at the Baltimore Museum of Art.

Massachusetts

In Boston, the Museum of Fine Arts has an exceptionally rich and varied collection of Homer's works and is a must for all serious admirers of this artist. Many outstanding oils, watercolors, and drawings from all periods are here, including a favorite oil painting, *Boys in a Pasture*. The Boston Public Library Rare Book Room also has a work by Homer. The Fogg Art Museum at Harvard University in nearby Cambridge has many Winslow Homer works, especially watercolors. The Mead Art Museum, Amherst College, has an oil, a watercolor, and some interesting drawings. The Addison Gallery of American Art at Phillips Academy, Andover, also has a rich collection of watercolors and drawings as well as two of Homer's finest oils, *Eight Bells* and *Kissing the Moon*. The Sterling and Francine Clark Art Institute, Williamstown, has many of Homer's watercolors and oils, including the famous *Two Guides* and *Undertow*, as well as an interesting series of sketches for the latter painting. The Worcester Art Museum also has an extensive collection, including Homer's prize-winning oil *The Gale*.

Other places to see Homer in Massachusetts include the Cape Ann Historical Association, Gloucester; Smith College Museum of Art, Northampton; and the Springfield Museum of Fine Arts.

Minnesota

The Minneapolis Institute of Arts has a fine watercolor, *Conch Divers*.

Mississippi

The Lauren Rogers Museum of Art, Laurel, has an oil painting called *Fisherman's Wife*.

Missouri

The Nelson Atkins Museum of Art in Kansas City and the St. Louis Art Museum have several Homers each. In the latter is the famous *The Country School*.

Nebraska

You can see a Homer drawing at the Sheldon Memorial Art Gallery, University of Nebraska, Lincoln, and the oil painting *Civil War Trooper, Soldier Meditating Beside a Grave* at the Joslyn Art Museum, Omaha.

New Hampshire

The Currier Gallery of Art, Manchester, has several watercolors.

New Jersey

The Montclair Art Museum, the Newark Museum, and the Plainfield Public Library all have several Homers. The Princeton University Art Museum and the Princeton University Library Rare Book Room both have at least one oil and a number of drawings and watercolors, including a charming one of Winslow Homer's sister-in-law, Alice Patch (Mrs. Arthur B.) Homer.

New York

New York City is an endless resource of art. The Metropolitan Museum of Art has one of the largest collections of art treasures in the world. You could spend weeks or even years here, looking at masterpieces from all parts of the globe. But you will find Winslow Homer's works in a part of the museum that is called the American Wing, which is on the second floor of the museum. Here you will find some of his great oil paintings: *Snap the Whip, The Gulf Stream,* and *The Carnival,* among others. This museum also has a number of Homer's brilliant watercolors from Nassau and Florida.

Some of Homer's finest watercolors are in the Brooklyn Museum, including *Fresh Air, Bear and Canoe, Glass Windows, The Unruly Calf, Shooting the Rapids, Jumping Trout, The Turtle Pound,* and many others. Here you can also see several fine oil paintings and drawings from various periods in Homer's career.

At the Cooper-Hewitt Museum you will find some fine oil and watercolor paintings as well as over 300 sketches—probably the largest collection of Homer's sketches in this country. Many of these are from his Civil War period, when he was following the troops on assignment for *Harper's Weekly.*

The National Academy of Design, the Museum of the City of New York, and the Whitney Museum of American Art also have some of Homer's works and *Harper's* engravings.

In the Adirondack Museum, Blue Mountain Lake, you can see a fine watercolor, *Casting, "A Rise."* One version of the oil painting *Croquet Players* is at the Albright-Knox Gallery, Buffalo, as well as a watercolor. The Canajoharie Library and Art Museum has about a dozen very fine watercolors and several oils as well as some drawings. The Hyde Collection in Glen Falls, The Memorial Art Gallery at the University of Rochester, the Parrish Art Museum in Southampton, the Everson Museum of Art in Syracuse, and the West Point Museum, United States Military Academy in West Point, also have some of Homer's works.

North Carolina

The North Carolina Museum of Art in Raleigh has an especially appealing oil painting, *Weaning the Calf.*

Ohio

The Cincinnati Art Museum, the Toledo Museum of Art, and the Cleveland Museum of Art all have good collections of Homer's works. The Butler Institute of American Art in Youngstown has one fine version in oil of *Snap the Whip,* plus a study for this painting.

Oklahoma

The Thomas Gilcrease Institute of American History and Art, Tulsa, has an oil painting by Homer.

Pennsylvania

In Philadelphia the Pennsylvania Academy of the Fine Arts has *The Fox Hunt*, the biggest oil painting Homer ever did and one of his finest. The Philadelphia Museum of Art has a fairly large collection of Homer's watercolors. The Carnegie Museum of Art in Pittsburgh also has a number of good watercolors and drawings as well as the important oil painting *The Wreck.* There is one watercolor at the Reading Public Museum and Art Gallery.

Rhode Island

The Museum of Art, Rhode Island School of Design in Providence, has a choice group of watercolors and drawings as well as several oils, including *Fishin'* and *On a Lee Shore*, which Homer himself described as "a very excellent painting."

Tennessee

The Hunter Museum of Art, Chattanooga, has a lovely watercolor, *Girl on Swing,* and the Memphis Brooks Museum of Art, Memphis, has *Reading by the Brook.*

Texas

You can find some of Homer's works at: The Dallas Museum of Fine Arts; the Amon Carter Museum, Fort Worth; the Museum of Fine Arts, Houston; and the McNay Art Museum, San Antonio.

Vermont

The Shelburne Museum has an oil painting, *Milking*, and the Robert Hull Fleming Museum, at the University of Vermont in Burlington, has *The Tent*, a well-known painting, and also a drawing.

Virginia

The Maier Museum of Art at Randolph-Macon Woman's College, Lynchburg, has the oil painting *Paris Courtyard.*

Washington

The Henry Art Gallery, University of Washington in Seattle, has a lovely oil painting, *An Adirondack Lake.*

West Virginia

The Huntington Museum of Art has a watercolor.

Wisconsin

The Milwaukee Art Center has a well-known painting from Homer's Tynemouth period, *Hark! The Lark!* The Paine Art Center and Arboretum, Oshkosh, has a watercolor.

IMPORTANT DATES IN THE LIFE OF HOMER

1836   February 24, Winslow Homer is born in Boston, Massachusetts, to Charles Savage Homer and Henrietta Maria Benson Homer.

1842   The Homer family moves to Cambridge.

1855   Homer is apprenticed to J. H. Bufford, lithographer in Boston.

1857   His apprenticeship to Bufford ends. Homer becomes a free-lance illustrator, doing work for *Harper's Weekly* and *Ballou's Pictorial Drawing Room Companion.*

1859   Homer moves to New York City, and continues to work with *Harper's Weekly.*

1860   He exhibits work for the first time at the National Academy of Design.

1861   As artist-correspondent for *Harper's Weekly,* Homer spends some time in Virginia with the Army of the Potomac. He takes a few lessons in oil painting.

1862   He spends time in Washington and Virginia with the Union Army on the Peninsula Campaign, sketching for *Harper's Weekly,* and does his first serious oil painting, *The Sharpshooter.*

1864   Homer is elected associate member of the National Academy of Design, and exhibits there regularly.

1865   He is elected a full Academician of the National Academy of Design.

1866   *Prisoners from the Front,* his first important oil painting, is shown to great acclaim.

1867   Two paintings are exhibited at the International Exposition in Paris. Homer goes to paint in Paris and Picardy.

1868   Back in the United States, Homer continues his illustrating work, but begins to take trips to New Hampshire to paint outdoor subjects. His French paintings are shown at the National Academy of Design.

1869   He visits the Jersey Shore, and paints *Long Branch, New Jersey.*

1872   He completes and shows several Hurley works, including *The Country School,* and finishes two versions of *Snap the Whip.*

1874   Homer exhibits his Gloucester watercolors to moderate acclaim. He spends time in the Adirondacks and visits the Valentines in Walden, New York.

1875   He goes back to Virginia to observe and paint scenes of African-American life, visits Prout's Neck, and exhibits *Breezing Up* (or *A Fair Wind*) to great acclaim.

1876   He visits the Valentines' Houghton Farm in Mountainville.

1879   The Houghton Farm works are shown at the American Water Color Society; they are highly praised.

1881–
1882   Homer sails to England and settles in Cullercoats, Tynemouth. He works in watercolors and makes sketches and drawings for future oils. New, more serious subject matter begins to appear in his work. Some works are exhibited at the Royal Academy in London, England. He returns to New York.

1883   Some of his Tynemouth watercolors are shown, but receive only a lukewarm reaction. *The Coming Away of the Gale* is poorly received at the National Academy. Homer visits the Jersey Shore to do studies for *Lifeline,* and arranges to move to Prout's Neck.

1884   Homer's mother dies. He sails to the Grand Banks with the fishing fleet, and visits Nassau and the Bahamas in December.

1885   He spends the winter in Nassau and Cuba, doing watercolors.

1886   Homer visits Florida and Key West, and paints watercolors. He completes and shows *Eight Bells* and *Undertow.*

1888   *Eight Bells* is exhibited at the National Academy of Design, and is very much admired.

1891   Homer revisits the Adirondacks, and paints many fine hunting scenes.

1893   Fifteen pictures are shown at the Columbian Exposition in Chicago; *The Gale* receives a gold medal. *The Fox Hunt* is exhibited in Philadelphia. Homer makes his first trip to Quebec.

1895   He finishes *Cannon Rock* and *The Northeaster*, important Maine Coast oils.

1896   *The Wreck* wins a five-thousand-dollar prize at the Carnegie Institute (Pittsburgh, Pennsylvania) exhibition.

1898   He has a two-man show with the artist George Inness at the Union League Club in New York, and gets rave reviews. Homer's father dies in Prout's Neck.

1899   Homer makes a January trip to Nassau. Back in Prout's Neck, he begins *The Gulf Stream.* In December he goes to Bermuda to do watercolors.

1900   Four paintings are exhibited at the Paris Exposition; *Summer Night* is awarded a gold medal, and is bought by the French government. Homer is awarded the Temple Gold Medal of the Pennsylvania Academy of the Fine Arts for *Northeaster*.

1906   The artist is unable to work for a long period because of ill health. The Metropolitan Museum of Art buys *The Gulf Stream.*

1908   Homer suffers a paralytic stroke in May. He makes a partial recovery, but will be ill for the rest of his life. He works on *Left and Right*, and visits the Adirondacks.

1909   He finishes his last oil painting, *Driftwood.*

1910   Homer dies in his studio at Prout's Neck on September 29.

Works Reproduced in This Book

This list of the works of Winslow Homer that are reproduced in this book tells the title, medium, and date of each, as well as where it can be found. Dimensions are given, height by width, in inches and in centimeters.

Front Jacket
Berry Pickers (detail). 1873. Pencil, watercolor, and gouache; 9¾ x 13⅞ in. (24.8 x 35.2 cm.). Collection of Mr. and Mrs. Paul Mellon, Upperville, Virginia.

Title page
"Gloucester Harbor" (detail). From *Harper's Weekly,* September 27, 1873.

Pages 4–5
The Country School. 1871. Oil on canvas, 21⅜ x 38⅜ in. (54.3 x 97.5 cm.). St. Louis Art Museum.

Page 6
Portrait of Winslow Homer at Prout's Neck. Silver print. Photograph by Peter Juley. Bowdoin College Museum of Art, Brunswick, Maine. Gift of the Homer Family.

Page 8
Boys in a Pasture. 1874. Oil on canvas, 15¼ x 22½ in. (38.7 x 57.1 cm.). Museum of Fine Arts, Boston. The Hayden Collection.

Page 9
Portrait of Arthur B. Homer. 1853. Pencil drawing, 10 x 8 in. (25.4 x 20.3 cm.). Private collection.

Page 11
"Corner of Winter, Washington and Summer Streets, Boston." Wood engraving. Front page of *Ballou's Pictorial*, June 13, 1857.

Pages 12–13
"Low Tide" (detail). Wood engraving. From *Every Saturday,* August 6, 1870.

Croquet Scene. 1866. Oil on canvas, 15⅞ x 26¹⁄₁₆ in. (40.4 x 66.1 cm.). Photography copyright © 1992 Art Institute of Chicago. Friends of American Art Collection, 1942.35.

Page 15
"The Army of the Potomac—A Sharpshooter on Picket Duty." Wood engraving, 9⅛ x 13¾ in. (23.2 x 34.9 cm.). From *Harper's Weekly,* November 15, 1862.

Pages 16–17
Prisoners from the Front. 1866. Oil on canvas, 24 x 38 in. (61 x 96.5 cm.). The Metropolitan Museum of Art, New York, New York. Gift of Mrs. Frank B. Porter, 1922.

Page 18
Winslow Homer and Albert Kelsey in Paris. 1867. Photograph, 5¾ x 4 in. (14.6 x 10.2 cm.). Bowdoin College Museum of Art, Brunswick, Maine. Gift of the Homer Family.

Page 19
"A Parisian Ball—Dancing at the Mabille, Paris." Wood engraving, 9⅛ x 13¾ in. (23.2 x 34.9 cm.). From *Harper's Weekly,* November 23, 1867.

Page 20
Eugène Boudin, *Beach at Trouville.* 1865. Oil on canvas, 15 x 24.1 in. (38 x 62.8 cm.). The Art Museum, Princeton University, Princeton. Gift of the estate of Laurence Hutton, 1913.

Page 21
Long Branch, New Jersey. 1869. Oil on canvas. 15 x 21¾ in. (38.1 x 54.6 cm.). Museum of Fine Arts, Boston. The Hayden Collection.

Page 22
An Adirondack Lake. 1870. Oil on canvas, 24¼ x 38¼ in. (61.6 x 97.2 cm.). Henry Art Gallery, University of Washington. Horace C. Henry Collection. Photograph by Steven J. Young.

Page 23
"Ship-Building, Gloucester Harbor." Wood engraving, 9⅜ x 13¾ in. (23.7 x 34.9 cm.). From *Harper's Weekly*, October 11, 1873.

Page 24
"Sea-Side Sketches—A Clam Bake" (detail). Wood engraving. From *Harper's Weekly*, August 23, 1873.

Pages 24–25
October Day. 1889. Watercolor, 13⅞ x 19¾ in. (35.8 x 50.2 cm.). Sterling and Francine Clark Art Institute, Williamstown, Massachusetts.

Page 26
"Gathering Berries." Wood engraving. *Harper's Weekly,* July 11, 1874.

Page 27
Berry Pickers. 1873. Pencil, watercolor, and gouache; 9¾ x 13⅞ in. (24.8 x 35.2 cm.). Collection of Mr. and Mrs. Paul Mellon, Upperville, Virginia.

Page 28

"Flirting on the Seashore and on the Meadow" (detail). Wood engraving. From *Harper's Weekly,* September 19, 1874.

Page 29

Fresh Air. 1878. Watercolor over charcoal, 20$\frac{1}{16}$ x 14$\frac{1}{16}$ in. (51 x 35.7 cm.). The Brooklyn Museum. Dick S. Ramsay Fund, 41.1087.

Page 30

Breezing Up (A Fair Wind). 1876. Oil on canvas, 24 x 38 in. (61.5 x 96.5 cm.). National Gallery of Art, Washington. Gift of the W. L. and May T. Mellon Foundation.

Page 31

Cotton Pickers. 1876. Oil on canvas, 24 x 38 in. (61 x 96.5 cm.). Los Angeles County Museum of Art. Acquisition made possible through Museum Trustees.

Page 33

Winslow Homer's Studio at Prout's Neck. Photograph, 10 x 7 in. (25.4 x 17.8 cm.). Bowdoin College Museum of Art, Brunswick, Maine. Gift of the Homer Family.

Page 34

Flamborough Head. 1882. Watercolor, 17$\frac{4}{5}$ x 24 in. (45.2 x 61 cm.). Photography copyright © 1992 Art Institute of Chicago. Mr. and Mrs. Martin A. Ryerson Collection, 1933.1240.

Page 35

Four Fishwives. 1881. Watercolor, 18 x 28$\frac{1}{2}$ in. (45.7 x 72.4 cm.). Galleries of the Claremont Colleges, Claremont, California. Scripps College, Gift of General and Mrs. Edward Clinton Young.

Pages 36–37

The Gale. 1883–1893. Oil on canvas, 30$\frac{1}{4}$ x 48$\frac{5}{16}$ in. (76.8 x 122.7 cm.). Worcester Art Museum, Worcester, Massachusetts.

Page 38

Charles Savage Homer, Jr., and Winslow Homer after Fishing. c. 1900. Photograph, 4$\frac{3}{4}$ x 6$\frac{11}{16}$ in. (12 x 17 cm.). Bowdoin College Museum of Art, Brunswick, Maine. Gift of the Homer Family, 1964.

Page 39

Corn Roast, Prout's Neck. c. 1880. Bowdoin College Museum of Art, Brunswick, Maine. Gift of the Homer Family.

Page 40
The Lifeline. 1884. Oil on canvas, 29 x 45 in. (73.7 x 114.3 cm.). Philadelphia Museum of Art. The George W. Elkins Collection.

Page 41
The Gulf Stream. 1889. Oil on canvas, 28⅛ x 49⅛ in. (71.4 x 124.8 cm.). The Metropolitan Museum of Art, Wolfe Fund, 1906. Catherine Lorillard Wolfe Collection.

Page 42
Eight Bells. 1886. Oil on canvas, 25¼ x 30⅛ in. (64.1 x 76.5 cm.). Copyright © Addison Gallery of American Art, Phillips Academy, Andover, Massachusetts. Gift of anonymous donor.

Pages 44–45
The Fox Hunt. 1893. Oil on canvas, 38 x 68½ in. (96.5 x 172.8 cm.). Pennsylvania Academy of the Fine Arts, Philadelphia. Joseph E. Temple Fund.

Page 46
"Dad's Coming" (detail). Wood engraving. From *Harper's Weekly,* November 1, 1873.

Page 47
"Dad's Coming" (detail).

Page 48
The Northeaster. 1895. Oil on canvas, 34⅜ x 50¼ in. (87.2 x 127.6 cm.). Metropolitan Museum of Art. Gift of George A. Hearn, 1910.

Page 50
Winslow Homer with *The Gulf Stream,* in his Prout's Neck studio. 1898. Photograph, 4¹¹⁄₁₆ x 6¾ in. (11.9 x 17.1 cm.). Bowdoin College Museum of Art, Brunswick, Maine. Gift of Elizabeth McLaren Stovel, Anne McLaren Griffin, and Donald McLaren in memory of their parents, Thayer and Madeleine Skinner McLaren.

Page 56
Winslow Homer (Bautain, Paris). 1866–1867. Photograph. Bowdoin College Museum of Art, Brunswick, Maine.

Page 59
"Our National Winter Exercise—Skating." Wood engraving. From *Frank Leslie's Illustrated Newspaper*, January 13, 1866.

Page 64
"Snap the Whip." Wood engraving. From *Harper's Weekly*, September 20, 1873.

First published in the United States of America in 1993 by
Rizzoli International Publications, Inc.
300 Park Avenue South
New York, New York 10010

Copyright © 1993 Rizzoli International Publications, Inc.

Library of Congress Cataloging-in-Publication Data

Beneduce, Ann.
    A weekend with Winslow Homer / by Ann Keay Beneduce
     p. cm.
    Summary: American painter Winslow Homer talks about his life and
work as if entertaining the reader for the weekend. Includes
reproductions of the artist's works and a list of museums where they
are on display.
    ISBN 0-8478-1622-2
    1. Homer, Winslow, 1836–1910—Juvenile literature. 2. Artists—
Unites States—Biography—Juvenile literature. [1. Homer,
Winslow, 1836–1910. 2. Artists.] I. Title.
ND237.H7B46   1993
759. 13—dc20   93-12189
                                      CIP
                                      AC

Design by Mary McBride
Editors: Lois Brown
       Isabelle Bleecker

Printed in Italy